MEET
Viola Desmond

ELIZABETH
MacLeod

ILLUSTRATED BY
MIKE DEAS

Scholastic Canada Ltd.
Toronto New York London Auckland Sydney
Mexico City New Delhi Hong Kong Buenos Aires

It was a cold, rainy day in November 1946. Viola Desmond needed to make a business trip. From her home in Halifax, she had to drive across Nova Scotia to Sydney.

It would not be pleasant to drive on such a wet day. But when Viola made up her mind to do something, she did it.

2

Viola had grown up in a big family, with ten brothers and sisters! Viola was one of the oldest. Her big sister Helen liked to bake. Viola would make the icing. Little sister Wanda helped too.

Viola's father had worked several jobs to support his family, including cutting hair. Maybe that's why Viola had decided to open a hair salon when she grew up.

3

It had been tough for Viola to get started. She had to go to Montreal to attend beauty school. No school in Halifax would train her because she was black.

When Viola came back home, she opened her own hair salon. Soon she had many customers.

4

Viola's customers loved visiting her salon because she was smart, caring and funny. Her customers were black women, who weren't allowed to go to the salons in Halifax that white women used.

Viola also made her own hair creams and face powders and started a beauty school to train other hairdressers.

On the way to Sydney, Viola's car began making terrible noises. The town of New Glasgow was just ahead. Viola pulled off the road to find some help.

Then Viola saw a movie theatre nearby. She decided to watch a movie in New Glasgow while she waited for her car. It was a decision that would shape Canada's history.

She walked into the theatre's main floor and sat down. It felt good to relax in a warm, dry place.

Viola snuggled down into her seat. The movie was just about to begin.

Suddenly, there was a tap on her shoulder.

Viola had been given a ticket for the balcony. The usher told her to move. Viola didn't want to sit in the balcony.

She went back to the ticket seller and asked again for a ticket on the main floor, even though it cost more.

The ticket seller refused. She said nothing about the colour of Viola's skin. But Viola knew that's what she meant.

That made Viola angry. When she went to the movies in Halifax, black people sat wherever they liked, just like white people. Viola marched back to the main floor and sat down.

11

But Viola had hardly sat down before the usher came back.

Then the manager came. But Viola stayed in her seat. Because when she made up her mind to do something, she did it!

A few minutes later, the manager was back with a police officer.

Viola was driven to the jail and put in a cell. A police officer shut the door with a loud clang. Then she turned the key.

CLICK

Some people might have cried. Not Viola. She was bruised and upset but she pulled on her white gloves.

With her back straight, Viola sat down on the bed. She sat there all night long and didn't sleep a wink.

The next morning, Viola was taken from her cell straight to a courtroom. The theatre manager, ticket seller, usher and police officer were all there.

Viola wasn't told that she could have a lawyer to help her, or more time to prepare. She didn't know she could ask questions.

The judge found Viola guilty. She hadn't paid that one cent of tax.

She was ordered to pay a fine of $26. That would be about $350 today.

No one said anything about the colour of Viola's skin. But everyone knew that's what this case was really about.

As Viola walked out of the courtroom she was angry. Her car was fixed and waiting for her at the garage. But Viola was too upset to drive to Sydney. She headed home.

Some of her friends said she should hire a lawyer and fight. They thought she could help change things for black Canadians.

Others said Viola should pretend the whole thing never
happened. Even her husband told her she should accept that black
people would always be treated badly.

One of Viola's customers, Carrie Best, ran a newspaper called the *Clarion*. It was Nova Scotia's first newspaper that was owned by black people.

The *Clarion* ran articles about what had happened to Viola. More people started to say Viola had been treated unfairly.

Viola decided to take her case to the top court in Nova Scotia. The Nova Scotia Association for the Advancement of Coloured People (NSAACP) agreed to help her.

They collected money to pay for a lawyer. Many people, black and white, gave money to help.

Viola was worried about going to court again, but she was determined, and this time she wasn't alone. Her lawyer and Carrie Best were with her.

But the judges at the top court would not hear Viola's case. They said she had waited too long to bring it to court.

Again, no one talked about the colour of Viola's skin.
But everyone knew that's what the case was still about.
One of the judges even hinted that the case wasn't really about that one cent of tax. He suggested it was about keeping black people apart from white people.

Viola knew she'd been treated badly because she was black. She hadn't won her court case, but the NSAACP kept working for justice. So did others, like Carrie Best and the *Clarion*.

A few years later, Viola moved to Montreal, where she took a business course. Then Viola headed to New York City, where she worked finding jobs for singers and actors. Viola died there in 1965.

But that's not the end of Viola's story.

When Viola spent that night in jail, her little sister Wanda had been ashamed.

But when Wanda was much older, she felt proud of Viola. Wanda was glad her sister had stood up for black Canadians.

Wanda began telling people Viola's story. She talked to children in schools. She spoke at universities. She gave interviews to reporters.

When people heard what had happened to Viola, they said it was unfair.

In 2010, Nova Scotia premier Darrell Dexter apologized to Viola and all black people in the province.

A pardon had been granted for Viola. He said she was not guilty of any crime. He said she had not been treated fairly.

Viola was the first Canadian ever to receive a pardon after she had died.

When it was announced that Viola was going to be put on Canada's ten-dollar bill, Wanda was so proud.

Viola had wanted to make things better and more fair for black Canadians. And she did.

Because when Viola made up her mind to do something, she did it!

Viola Desmond's Life

July 6, 1914   Viola Irene Davis is born in Halifax, Nova Scotia.

1930s   Viola receives training in beauty care in Montreal, Atlantic City, New Jersey and New York City.

1936   Viola marries Jack Desmond.

1937   Viola opens her own hair salon in Halifax. It is called Vi's Studio of Beauty Culture.

VIOLA IN HER HALIFAX SALON, ABOUT 1938.

VIOLA (RIGHT) AND HER SISTER WANDA, ABOUT 1950.

November 8, 1946   Viola is arrested at the Roseland Theatre in New Glasgow, Nova Scotia.

November 9, 1946   Viola is found guilty of not paying the province of Nova Scotia one cent of tax.

January 20, 1947	The Nova Scotia Supreme Court refuses to hear Viola's case.
Late 1940s	Viola moves to Montreal.
1950s	Viola moves to New York City.
February 7, 1965	Viola dies in New York City.
April 15, 2010	Viola is granted a pardon.
February 1, 2012	Viola appears on a Canadian stamp.
November 15, 2017	Viola receives a star on Canada's Walk of Fame in Toronto.
Fall 2018	Viola appears on Canada's ten-dollar bill. She is the first Canadian woman to appear alone on the front of a banknote.

THIS POSTAGE STAMP WAS ISSUED FOR BLACK HISTORY MONTH IN 2012.

VIOLA'S SISTER WANDA ROBSON (LEFT) LOOKS ON AS LIEUTENANT GOVERNOR OF NOVA SCOTIA MAYANN FRANCIS SIGNS VIOLA'S PARDON.

With lots of love to my great niece and nephew Madeline and Gregory
Sumner. I hope there always will be justice and fairness in your lives.

— E.M.

For Annie and Faye.

— M.D.

Many thanks to editor Erin O'Connor for her hard work, and to the
whole team at Scholastic. Thanks also to my brothers John and Douglas,
and to Paul for his support in all my battles.

— E.M.

Scholastic Canada Ltd.
604 King Street West, Toronto, Ontario M5V 1E1, Canada

Scholastic Inc.
557 Broadway, New York, NY 10012, USA

Scholastic Australia Pty Limited
PO Box 579, Gosford, NSW 2250, Australia

Scholastic New Zealand Limited
Private Bag 94407, Botany, Manukau 2163, New Zealand

Scholastic Children's Books
Euston House, 24 Eversholt Street, London NW1 1DB, UK

www.scholastic.ca

The illustrations were created using a blend of digital tools with traditional media.
Sketches were created with a Wacom tablet and Photoshop, then traced onto watercolour
paper, where colour and texture were added using gouache and watercolour paints.
Ink was used to add the black line to finish the art.

Photos ©: cover and title page speech bubble, top right: fatmayilmaz/iStockphoto;
30 left: Viola Desmond in Her Studio, ca. 1938, Wanda Robson & Viola Desmond Collection,
Sydney, NS, Item #16-87-30227, Beaton Institute, Cape Breton University;
30 right: Hi-Hat Club, Boston, ca. 1950, Wanda Robson & Viola Desmond Collection,
Sydney, NS, Item #16-93-30233, Beaton Institute, Cape Breton University;
31 top: Canada Post © 2012, reprinted with permission; 31 bottom:
Andrew Vaughan/Canadian Press Images.

Library and Archives Canada Cataloguing in Publication

MacLeod, Elizabeth, author
    Meet Viola Desmond / Elizabeth MacLeod ; illustrated by Mike Deas.

(Scholastic Canada biography)
ISBN 978-1-4431-1351-9 (softcover).--ISBN 978-1-4431-6387-3 (hardcover)

    1. Desmond, Viola, 1914-1965--Juvenile literature. 2. Race discrimination--
Nova Scotia--History--Juvenile literature.   3. Civil rights--Nova Scotia--History--
Juvenile literature. 4. Black Canadians--Nova Scotia--Biography--Juvenile
literature. 5. Biographies. I. Deas, Mike, 1982-, illustrator II. Title.

FC2346.26.D48M34 2018   j971.6'004960092   C2017-907349-4

6 5 4 3 2 1   Printed in Malaysia 108   18 19 20 21 22